William R. Cox

General Hints on House Painting

Containing Practical Rules and Information on the Subject of Paints and

Painting

William R. Cox

General Hints on House Painting
Containing Practical Rules and Information on the Subject of Paints and Painting

ISBN/EAN: 9783337064242

Printed in Europe, USA, Canada, Australia, Japan

Cover: Foto ©Lupo / pixelio.de

More available books at **www.hansebooks.com**

ON

HOUSE PAINTING:

CONTAINING

Practical Rules and Information

ON THE SUBJECT OF

PAINTS AND PAINTING,

FOR THE

JOURNEYMAN, THE APPRENTICE AND THE INEXPERIENCED.

BY WM. R. COX.

CINCINNATI:

—

1872.

INTRODUCTION.

To our Patrons and the Public.

IN presenting the following general hints on House Painting, Varnishing, etc., to our customers and the public, we have only to remark that they are entirely practical, and are written with the view of supplying information, such as we are called upon to furnish daily. We make no attempt at technical description, but confine ourselves exclu ively to such wording as the simplest may understand. There has been more pretentious works issued on the subject of paints and painting, but we have looked in them in vain for such hints as the everyday workman requires. The rules we lay down here are those that we follow ourselves, and have followed during the past twenty-five years.

With the aid of instructions conveyed in this little book, we believe the most inexperienced will be able to go about a job of painting with a knowledge sufficient to turn out a fair specimen of work. We do not propose to make finished artists, for they are even rare in the house painting profession; but if we enable our readers to do better work with our hints than they could do without them, it is all that we hope for or claim.

Very respectfully,

WM. R. COX & CO.

GENERAL HINTS ON HOUSE PAINTING.

TO MIX ANY ORDINARY COLOR—SAY, WHITE.

Take from your keg of pure white lead (no other should be used) as much as you think will do the work you wish to do. Then add as much Japan dryer as will dry it in twenty-four hours, which, if it is a good article, will be, say a large teaspoonful to the pound of white lead, if it be warm weather; but if cold or damp weather, a much larger portion, say a tablespoonful, will be necessary. Then thoroughly mix by stirring it with the lead until every particle of the brown color of the Japan has been obliterated from the top of the lead, being careful to stir the lead up around the sides of your paint-pot, so as not to leave a particle of the Japan to show either on the top of the lead or on the sides of the pot. If the work you are doing is inside work, and is the priming or first coat, you will then add of pure raw linseed oil and turpentine mixed, of the proportion of three quarts of oil to one quart of turpentine, a small quantity to your pot of color, and before stirring wash the paint stick and sides of the pot thoroughly with a brush, in order to remove all the thick lead and Japan from the sides. The object of this is to first get all the lead into one compact mass, or of an even consistency, and second (and which is of the greatest importance to new beginners), to induce habits of cleanliness in working their pots and tools.

After washing off all color from the sides of your pot, rendering it perfectly clean, you will then stir the lead with the thinners* added until it is incorporated. If the color be too thick for use, add more, and stir until you make it of the proper consistency. If for priming on new work, your color

*The word thinners is the technical term applied to oil and turpentine when mixed together, and where both are to be applied at one and the same time.

should be thinned until it is as limpid as skim milk; but if for second coating, or for a covering of work that has been previously painted, and you wish to renew it, your color should be of the consistency of thick cream.

After having your color prepared and ready for application, first remove all dirt, sand or mortar (should there be any) from the surface by rubbing it with No. 1 or 1½ sandpaper. Then apply your paint in the following manner:

If it be a door or window frame, begin at the bottom of one side, painting upward, being sure to cover the entire surface evenly by rubbing your color out with the brush until you have covered every quirk, bead or angle. Then lay off your work by drawing the brush from the bottom upward, being careful in handling your tools, so as not to flirt or throw the color from your brush on the floor.

Continue on your next stretch or space, standing clear of the frame as far as you can reach. When this latter portion of the frame is done, lay it off by drawing your brush from the top of your stretch downward until it completely covers or laps on to what was first done. If your work shows any brush or bristle-marks, you will gently touch the point of your brush (which should by this time be almost free of color) to the work, striking it lightly over the face of the frame, right and left.

The best guide to go by in laying off work, is to always finish or lay off the work so as to run with the grain of the wood. After doing your second stretch, if your work be not done to the top of the frame, continue in the same manner to the top. Then do the top to the other side, and downward to the bottom. When reaching the floor, cut close to it with the point of your brush. When finished, if any portion of the paint has touched the floor, carefully remove it with your putty knife (by the way, that and one other tool—a simple ladder-hook—composes the entire stock of tools required by a painter, and he should never be without them). If you have by accident allowed any of the paint to splatter upon the floor, carefully remove every one of the stains by rubbing them off with sandpaper; or if they be small, with the ball of the foot. Follow the same rules until all the work you propose doing is complete.

TO PAINT OR PRIME A DOOR.

Clean off as first directed. If there be any spots of dirt or dust, paint the two top panels first, being careful to thoroughly fill every quirk or angle in the moulding around it, and take care not to let too much color get in the quirks or angles. Then the two bottom ones, then your meeting or up and down rails between panels; then your lock rail, your top and bottom rails, and lastly your side rails, being careful to at all times apply your color evenly, and to lay off each rail with the course of the grain of the wood, to make a closely defined and evenly cut dividing line between the course of the cross rails and the up and down rails. If you should do so, carefully wipe it all out with a dry brush, or your sash-tool. Then lay off carefully as before directed.

TO PAINT A WINDOW.

First find if your sash are hung on cord, or are provided with catches. If the former, run down the top sash until even with the sill, then carefully remove all dirt or soot from the runs of the sash (commonly called pulley stiles); then clean your sash with a duster, carefully removing all dirt from the corners. Then shove the inside or bottom sash up so as to entirely cover all but the top rail of the top sash; then take your sash-tool and carefully trace each light, commencing at the three top lights, if there be that many. Then the three lower ones; then run around the entire rail of the sash, taking special care not to let your brush touch the pulley stiles, as the paint not only prevents the sash from running smoothly, but is a sure indication of a slovenly or careless workman. After doing this, shove the top sash half way up the window, and pull the top one down until the bottom of it has cleared the top rail of the top sash. Then paint as you did the first part. Then examine the glass carefully, and wipe the surface of it all over, to be sure that you do not leave any spots of paint upon it. This being done, you will shove it up till within a half inch of the top of the window, that it may dry. Should you shove it clear up into the pulley stiles, and it remains long enough to become dry, it is likely to become stuck or glued fast by the paint on the sash. Do the bottom sash in precisely the same manner, with the exception that you will paint the top edge of your sash first. When finishing, do your frame around in the same manner as before. When the doors and frames are finished, you will (if there be one) do the cap of the base the same color; after that, paint the lower part of your base, and your room will be finished with the exception of the mantle. If there is one to be painted, proceed as follows:

The color will make no difference whatever as to the way work should be done, therefore we will say nothing about colors at present.

TO PAINT A MANTLE.

First thoroughly clean off the mantle, if it be required, dusting out the corners of the hearth, and remove all ashes and other refuse matter. Brush all back from it so as to entirely clean the hearthstone, so as not to stir it up with your feet in working. With your sash-tool cut carefully around the bottom of the plinth or foot of the column of the mantle. Then carefully lay on your color to the cap of column, cutting the line between the plaster up to the top of shelf. Do the other column in like manner. When both are complete, do the under part of the shelf, and after this do the entire front. Lastly, clean off the top of the shelf, and your work is finished. This formula will apply to almost every species of house-painting.

SECOND COATING.

We will now suppose that the work you have just finished is the priming, or first coat, of an entirely new house, and that your intention is to finish it with but three coats of plain white. This being the case, the next thing is to prepare work for its second coat as follows: With some good, pure putty in the left hand, and a putty-knife in your right, fill up flush all nail holes and other imperfections in the following manner: Openings or cracks that may be found occasioned by the works not being properly put together, or from the shrinkage of green lumber; take particular care to fill up flush all hammer bruises or other imperfections to give the work a clean, uniform appearance. After the work is entirely puttied up, rub it clean and smooth with No. 1 sandpaper; a sheet of which tear in four equal parts, and then double each part as you use it with the sanded side outward, taking care to rub up and down or across, as the course of the grain of the wood may run. On all moulding or beads, double up or squeeze your paper so as to remove all particles of fuzz that may have been left by the joiner. When all is thoroughly cleaned, and the surface is perfectly smooth, remove all particles of dust that may have accumulated in using the paper; and after all the work in the room has been done to your satisfaction, and is ready for the second coat, prepare your color as before directed, with the exception, that as this is the second coat, it must necessarily be of a heavier body, or thicker than that used as priming—say as thick as good cream. When your color is ready, apply it as before directed, with the exception of being more careful in laying off your work than you was with the first coat, in order to give the surface as smooth an appearance as possible. After giving your work sufficient time to dry and become perfectly hard, proceed to again rub it off lightly with No. $\frac{1}{2}$ sandpaper, as it is much smoother and finer than No. 1, and is more suitable to make a smooth surface on fresh paint. Should you still find small holes or imperfections, putty them up as before, and run the sandpaper over the face of the new putty to take off any that may remain more than is necessary to make the work flush and smooth.

THIRD COATING.

In preparing the color for this coat, if you wish to make a nice job of it, and that it may remain white and clear, and not turn yellow from the warmth of the sun and air, take of the best French white zinc, ground in oil—say six pounds—and of the best pure white lead, three pounds; stir well together, and instead of using Japan for a dryer, add to the above ten pounds of color, about half a pound of the best English patent dryer, ground in oil, adding a little spirits of turpentine to assist you in more thoroughly mixing the dryer with the lead. Add a little more turpentine (no oil to be used in this coat, as it will surely turn yellow on the inside, or where it does not get light and air, just as the finest white linen will turn yellow by being excluded from the air for a long time in laying in a dark cupboard or drawer), and stir gently until the mixture is of an even consistency. When thin enough for use, strain it carefully through a fine brass wire strainer set over another pot to receive the strained color as it runs through. If the color is a little too thick to run through the strainer easily (which it should be), take your sash-tool and rub the surface of the wire until it is all through except the skins or dried particles of paint adhering to the sides of the keg. If lumps of imperfectly mixed lead remain in the strainer, put them back into the pot, and, with your paddle and a little spirits of turpentine, thoroughly crush them, and run them again through your strainer.

CLEANING THE MIXING POTS.

When thoroughly strained, wipe out the pot you mixed in first with a dry brush (one that you have wiped all of the color out of, by drawing it across the paint-stick, or over the edge of your pot). Then add a small amount of spirits, and, with your other brush, wash around the inside and outside of your pot, and across the wires of your strainer, in order to remove all the remaining thick paint, and to prevent the strainer and bucket from becoming useless. When you have got off all that can be washed off with spirits and the brush, take a small piece of soft rag (which you should always have with you), and wipe off the inside and outside of both strainer and pot, and with a stiff, short, clean duster, clean out all small particles of paint that yet remain in the meshes of the strainer. If you do not wish to use it, or the pot that you first mixed color in, for the present, hang each of them in their proper places to be ready for future use. Be particular to observe that the three great principles of any business, and upon which rest all the success any one may expect, are, first, economy in saving everything that can be made useful; second, cleanliness, that you may be always able to use any tool you want without the loss of time to clean it, when you are busy at something else; and, third, order, that you may be able to put your hands upon anything you want the moment it is desired.

READY FOR WORK.

Now having your color and brushes all clean and ready for use, you will proceed to apply it in the same manner as previous coats, taking renewed care in laying off your work and in handling your brush, so as not to splatter or throw your color (which from its being mixed entirely with spirits, has become very limpid or short), and to rub off or clean up all that may fall in working it.

Having finished your work with three good coats of white, you may desire to give it a gloss or varnish finish. Should this be the case, and you wish to make it a very white, clean job of work, give it a fourth coat of pure, white zinc, prepared in the same manner as the color for the third coat, with the exception that you now add as a portion of your thinners three fourths to one pint of pure white Damar varnish to help give it a body. The next, or fourth coat, apply as before, laying on your color very smooth and with a very light touch of the point of the brush to prevent brush-marks. (You will recollect that before applying additional coats of paint, the under or last coat has become thoroughly dry and hard.) After this fourth coat has stood long enough to become hard—say two days—you will take of pure French zinc, ground in Damar varnish, a sufficient quantity for the surface of the work to be glossed—say two pounds of the zinc lead to one fourth of a gallon (or even three pints is not too much if the lead be very heavy), and stir them well together. If it is cold weather and your varnish is heavy, add a very little turpentine to make it work free and prevent its being what is called ropy (or showing the large thick creases you sometimes see on work of this kind caused by being laid on too thick). Strain and again apply. This coat will now begin to show a beautiful white gloss or polish, but will, after it has set, look a little dead, on account of not having a sufficient body of varnish under it. When it has stood for a couple of days to dry, take what color there is left, if any, and add more varnish, so as to make it of the proportion of one and a half pounds of zinc lead, ground in Damar varnish, to one fourth of a gallon of clear Damar, adding also a little spirit to make it work free; again apply as before. If you have followed the directions strictly, you will find that you have as pretty a job of glossed white as can reasonably be wished for, and which will outwear anything that can be put on in the paint line.

TO MIX STONE COLOR.

To mix stone color, or any dark color, take of the best white lead ten pounds ; of pure yellow ochre ground in oil, two pounds ; of Venetian, one fourth of an ounce ; and of black, one fourth of an ounce. Stir well together. (Always stir coloring with the lead before adding any oil to it.) If it is too light, add a little more black by tipping the point of your paint-stick into it, and stirring until of a shade to suit. It is almost impossible to give a formula of any color that would give a specific quantity of each of its compounds, caused by the variation in strength of different colors. The same amount of a pure color mixed with another, as, for instance, an ounce of pure lampblack, will turn ten pounds of lead a very dark shade ; while a pound of an inferior black would not make the same quantity of lead half as dark. It would not be as clear and transparent as with the pure, but of a muddy, cloudy appearance. Drab color is mixed the same as stone color, with the exception that you add more yellow and red and less black. To make a light brown, add red shaded with brown till of a shade to suit.

WHITENING CEILINGS OR WALLS.

To whiten or color a ceiling or wall, place your trussel at one end of the room ; with a bucket of water remove every particle of smoke and soot, using for that purpose an old worn-out coloring brush ; sponge dry. If the ceiling has been previously whitened, remove every particle of it with brush and sponge ; or should it have been whitewashed or scaled, and is hard to remove, first remove all loose particles with a scraper, and then wash clean, as the cleaner you get it the less trouble you will have in making a good job of work. When the ceilings are thoroughly cleaned, prepare your color as follows: Take of best Gilder's whitening, ten pounds ; of best American zinc, dry, four to five pounds. Sift while dry through an ordinary flour seive, and mix with water as thick as you can possibly make it. Put a half pound of good ordinary white glue in a pot, and pour enough cold water on it to cover it. Let it soak for an hour or so, then set it in a pan or pot of boiling water, and stir till entirely dissolved. While your glue is dissolving, take a half bar of ordinary brown soap, and shave it fine in a small quantity of warm water ;

set it on the stove to boil. When your soap and glue are ready, pour them into your bucket of whitening. If it is too thick, add a little cold water, if in warm weather, or a little warm water if cold or winter weather. If two persons are engaged, divide the color in two water buckets. Place a stick across the center of each bucket, by cutting it just long enough to press down tight about one inch below the top, as a rest for your brush when not in use, and to wipe out the superfluous color while using. When ready, both mount the scaffold, one at each end, and apply your color, laying it on smoothly and freely, being careful to cover every part of your work, taking a space as large as you can conveniently reach. Remove your scaffold to another stretch in same manner, repeating the operation until the entire ceiling is covered. If there is a cornice or ornaments to the room, after the flat surface is finished, give them a good coat of preparation, using a small three-inch flat brush for the purpose, and your small flat fitch to thoroughly color all the ornaments. When your ceiling has become dry—which in good dry weather will be almost as soon as you can go from one side of a ceiling to the other—if you have any of your first coating left, add enough of pure clean whitening and zinc to make the quantity desired. Add a very little white glue well dissolved, stir well together, and then thin with cold water until it is the consistency of milk. Go over your ceiling again, being careful as before to cover every particle of its surface. When dry, your ceiling will present a beautiful white appearance. Finish your cornice and center-piece, and your work is done.

To kalsomine or color walls use the same process precisely; shading your color or colors to suit the taste, and adding a larger solution of glue, in order to prevent its rubbing off. If your ceilings are very dirty and stained, as is sometimes the case, the addition of a little ultramarine blue will prove of great benefit in making your color cover and look solid and smooth.

TO MAKE TINTED COLORS.

To make different colors for walls, or tinted colors, as they are sometimes called, take of your whitening ready prepared for use. To make a pink, add enough of English or French vermillion, well worked in water, as will darken the color to four or five shades darker than you want it, when dry and in order. To get the color to suit you before applying, spread a small quantity of color on a piece of paper and lay it on the stove to dry. If it is not dark enough, add more red. When of the right shade, strain it through a paint-strainer, to get the color thoroughly mixed. Then apply as before described.

To make a French gray, add pure ultramarine blue, in quantity as your taste desires. Then add dry Indian red, well pulverized, to give it a delicate redish tint, but not enough to make it a purple; add, in very small quantities at a time, pure English drop black until your color is of that peculiar neutral tint in which the black, blue and red are so evenly blended that neither of them will predominate, and yet all of them can be detected. This will make what is called a French gray. Strain as before.

To make lavender, or lilac, take of best No. 40 carmine, dry enough to make your color as deep as you require. When thoroughly mixed, add enough of French ultramarine blue to let neither blue nor carmine predominate. If you wish it a warm tint, add but little blue, if a cold tint of lilac, add more blue until a required shade is reached, being careful, in every case, to strain your color before using, as if it is not perfectly mixed it is apt to look cloudy and streaked, and mars the beauty of the work.

All other shades, both in oil and water color, can be prepared to suit the taste in the same manner. If green is desired, and you want a very delicate tint, use the best Paris green to shade with; or, if a good strong durable green, use any of the best chrome greens, as magnesia or Marseilles. If brown, use Van Dyke or burnt umber, or red and black. If neither Van Dyke or umber are warm enough, and you want a very brilliant brown, warm up your color with a little English or French vermillion, or if you do not desire so expensive a color, use the ordinary Venetian red. If maroon color is wanted, use Indian red shaded with a little Prussian or celestial blue, shaded to suit. And so on through all the different combination of colors that could be thought of or desired.

TO MAKE GRAINING COLORS IN OIL.

If a light color is desired, take as much white lead as you require to do the work. Add yellow ochre until it is as dark as you want it; stir the Japan, wash down the sides of your pot, and add thinners till ready for use, and then apply. If you wish the base, or any portion of your work darker than the rest, add more ochre and a slight tint of Venetian red, till of the color required. This combination is universally used for graining. But, to make a nice, clean, clear color, take of white lead, ten lbs.; light chrome yellow, a half to one and three quarters lbs.; and of the best burnt sienna in oil as much as will take the sharpness off of the yellow, being careful to not get too much sienna in your color, as it will be apt to give your graining too fiery a cast. When ready, apply as before.

TO GRAIN OAK — TOOLS TO BE USED.

When your groundwork is properly finished and ready for graining, before applying your graining color, sandpaper the work thoroughly, to get it smooth and free from all roughness of the paint, and then prepare your graining color as follows : Pure burnt sienna, one lb.; raw umber, half lb.; beeswax dissolved in boiled oil, one ounce ; of pure whitening ground in oil, to lighten and make your color transparent, one half to three quarters lbs.; stir thoroughly together, and to the proper consistency, thus prepared, as follows : Of pure turpentine, three pints ; of boiled oil, one pint ; of Japan dryer, one half pint, thus—turpentine and Japan to be first well mixed to prevent curdling ; then add the oil, mixed well by shaking. When the color is ready for use, strain and apply. If too dark for the groundwork, add a little more sienna and whitening ; and if not dark or brown enough, add a little more umber ; and if raw umber does not give as brown a cast as you desire, add (thoroughly mixing) a little pure burnt umber, and see that all the ingredients are perfectly mixed. Strain again before using. Then, with a No. 7 or 8 sash-tool dipped in your color, apply some of it to the panel or such portion of the work you propose graining, and with a three and a half inch paste brush thoroughly distribute the color you have put on with the sash-tool until it has covered the entire panel, or such portion of it as you wish to cover; and so proceed until the entire side of door or the piece of work you propose doing is covered. If you wish to have a portion of panel or rail a little darker than another, as is often found in the natural wood, draw your sash-tool over the portion you wish to darken, and with your blending brush distribute the color evenly and smoothly. When finished and ready for the figuring, if you wish to imitate the heart of the wood, proceed with a piece of canton flannel of from four to six inches wide and twelve or fifteen long, one corner of which you will have drawn over the thumb, so that the nail may make the vein or imitation, being careful to shift the flannel over the thumb every moment or two so as to always have a clean portion just over the nail. Be sure at all times to have a clearly wiped out and distinct vein. Continue to add vein after vein until your piece of work has as many figures in it as you may think the work requires. Then with your coarse comb strike lightly over the work, being sure to draw your comb along the course the grain pursues, so as to give it an open, crooked appearance of the same figure of oak. Then, with a small camel's hair pencil and some thick graining color, delicately and neatly strike in the dark shades. Comb up the side of your panel, run around the moulding with the fine comb, and the panel will be ready for shading. You will then proceed with the next portion, or what is called a light imitation. Finish with your leather, or rubber comb carefully two-thirds of the panel. This will produce the carefully curved appearance of oak wood. Then comb the center a little finer, gently varying the course of the comb by holding it diagonally to the course of the grain to be made; then with your coarse and medium steel combs comb up the unfinished portion of the panel, being careful to let your lines gradually grow finer from the center or starting points until they are as fine as your first comb will make it, and with a flannel cloth wipe out the figures or grain of the wood, carefully imitating the pattern you have selected to copy. After completing your panels, do the meeting or cross rails, varying the style of pattern of figure as much as possible, to relieve the work of too much sameness, or too much of one figure, which does not look well.

To do graining you should have a full set of combs, consisting of a fine, a medium and a coarse comb, each of one, two, three and four inches wide, a good leather or India rubber comb, one side cut to grain a coarse line, and the other to grain a medium or fine line. A good grainer who knows how to handle and shape his comb to the work can make the first lines by simply modulating the course of his comb, as he draws it over his work. In addition to his set of combs, he wants a duster, a blender, a three and a half inch paste brush, a sash-tool, a top-grainer, two or three small pencils, and his sandpaper, to first smooth off the work before applying color.

SHADING.

After graining has become dry, if you wish to shade it, take a little thick umber and sienna mixed together upon a pallette board or a small piece of window glass, dip the point of your sash-tool into the color, and apply it to the portion of panel or rail you wish to shade; then with your blending brush carefully blend the color all over the part you want darkened, and carefully wipe out the portion you want to show light; and with your blender again soften down the edges of the shade, making a clean and distinct line on all portions of both rails and stiles, where they join each other, by laying the square edge of a piece of tin made for the purpose, or a piece of sandpaper, which is always most convenient and will answer as well. Then with your graining cloth wipe off all the shading color that may be left on the portion you wish left without the shade. Darken the mouldings, if there be any to the door or frame, to make a pleasant contrast. Leave work to dry.

Your work has now received three coats of graining color, and has been grained and shaded; the pores of the wood must necessarily be entirely filled from observation. Should it then require varnishing, you must use a first rate article, or your work will in a very short time be completely ruined by the cracking of the varnish.

QUALITY OF VARNISH.

Varnish sold by most of the drug stores is of the cheapest kind, and is not fit for anything that has ever had a coat of paint.

Not one dealer in a hundred knows enough of the nature of paint or varnish to give the purchaser the proper instructions as to what he should buy for his work. The purchaser does not require much, but wants a good article, and is willing to pay for it. Right here I may as well state the uses of the different varnishes and their names. First, or cheapest, sold by all dealers, is the No. 1 copal or furniture varnish. This is usually adulterated with rosin, and is almost worthless for any purpose, unless it be to fill up the pores of open grained woods by first applying it and afterward scraping it all off. Next, is the extra No. 1 copal, which is made of good, pure, selected gum-copal and made with care; when a really good article, it is the most serviceable varnish in use, and is used by all furniture makers for their first or filling-up coat, and upon which they rub and prepare their work, with the exception of the last or flowing coat, which is always of the best (or should be of the best) Zanzibar selected gum. The extra No. 1 copal can be used for all kinds of interior housework where the natural wood is used, and where the work does not come in contact with the sun, as with window sashes or inside shutters, or the outside of doors or frames. The best and surest varnish for all first or under coats of hard-wood finish, either interior or exterior, is the rubbing body or hard drying coach varnish. This varnish is prepared expressly as a foundation or filling varnish for coach work, with hard gum and a little oil, so as to admit of being easily rubbed down to a polishing surface. It also combines durability of wear with quick drying, and becomes hard enough to rub in from four to five days after the application of each coat. These qualities give it a superior advantage over all other varnishes made, and should at all times give it a decided preference over any other.

Where parties desire a good and lasting job of work, it must be borne in mind that the hard drying coach varnish should be finished with a flowing coat of the best Zanzibar, or the best flowing coach or English coach varnish, as a hard-drying varnish is capable of being rubbed to a polish, and not having as much oil in its combination as the flowing or finishing varnishes, is apt to go dead, or blind, if left to come in contact with the atmosphere. As our instructions in varnishing hard wood will cover that point, we will drop it here, and resume it under a more general heading.

In varnishing grained work, no one should think of using a No. 1 copal, as it is only a filling-up varnish, and from its liability to crack, would ruin any painted groundwork on which it is used, no matter how much boiled oil the painter may use with it—as is often practiced by unscrupulous and rascally men who have no regard for their reputation either for honesty or workmanship. This rascality is practiced every day in this and every other city in the country, and is encouraged by the owners of buildings and contractors, and by worthless stokers and deckhands on steamboats, who daub the spars and buckets with a simple mixture of boiled oil and white lead in any way that will cover the grain of the wood and make it look clean. These fellows, when their occupation is gone by the boat again resuming its regular trips, have the effrontery to apply to the first boss for a situation as a full-fledged painter. Being the busy season, and needing help, the boss puts one of these men (fresh from painting his last steamboat bucket) to work priming brick wall, or some other work that he cannot possibly spoil. The boss soon discovers who his new man is, but, as he is short of help, the man is retained as an assistant until the hurry is over, and is paid off at what he is worth. Having acquired another new idea of painting, the man engages with another boss for a day or two. It is often the case that he will not work for a boss more than an hour. (I have myself discharged and set to work three different men in an hour, all of them professing to fully understand the work.) By the time our amateur painter has been employed and discharged by five or six—possibly ten or twelve—shops, he has worked, in that time, say two weeks, and has had an opportunity to see the inside and outside finish of some pretty well painted houses, he considers his education in the painting business fully equal to the best workman in the city. As the busy season is ended, and he can no longer procure work, he is ready to start an establishment for himself.

Having no proper knowledge of the business, he purchases spurious drugs and inferior oils, makes cheap blind cash contracts, ruins half a dozen well painted houses, is found out, leaves his bills unpaid, and "jumps the town," to repeat the same course of daubing and rascality in another locality.

RESUME.—The painter, in order to make a good and permanent job of his graining, just done, must give it two good coats of varnish, as follows: the first coat should be of the best hard-drying or rubbing body coach, applied just thick enough to flow easily and smoothly. When the work is finished, it should be given at least one week to dry, before putting on the last coat. When ready for the last coat, the work should be smoothly rubbed down with very fine sandpaper or a bunch of haircloth, then well dusted off, and a first-rate flowing coat of the best flowing varnish, or if great durability is desired, finish with a coat of best medium drying English coach varnish. Much of the varnishing now done is finished with but one heavy coat of flowing varnish the first year, and is let stand until the next season, when the last or finishing coat is applied.

It would be almost impossible to go sufficiently into detail to give an accurate and intelligible description of all the different ways of doing the different kinds of graining now practiced, but if you wish to pursue the business of graining, the best course will be to connect yourself with a competent grainer, one well practiced in his business, and remain with him until you have a perfect knowledge of the business in all its branches. Rosewood, maple, black and white walnut, cherry, and mahogany, are nearly all done best in distemper or water colors. But as we have but little space left us, and all who have practiced graining to any extent know its uses and application, we will proceed

TO VARNISH ON THE NATURAL WOODS.

The painter or varnisher should at all times be careful to remove every stain or spot from his work before priming. Should he find any bruise or stain that he cannot remove, he should at once apply to the carpenter for assistance. When complete and clean, he should commence his work and complete it as follows: All white pine, cherry or maple should have three good coats of best rubbing body coach, or extra No. 1 copal varnish (the former being much more durable, and not so liable to crack or lose its polish as the latter); the work to be thoroughly and smoothly rubbed down with No. 0 sandpaper after applying each coat, except the last, or third coat, when there should be an interval of at least four or five days between the application of each coat, to enable the under coat to get thoroughly dry. The varnish should be as heavy, and applied as freely, as the judgment of the varnisher (which experience only can teach) will permit, after the last coat has stood not less than four days. (It would be better if it stood ten.) The surface should be rubbed down with a haircloth rubber and No.½, or not coarser than No. 1, pulverized pummice stone and water until it has received a perfectly smooth, even surface. Now lay aside your haircloth rubber, and, with a rubber made of woollen cloth, rub the entire surface of the work with a little pummice stone and water, gradually working the pummice stone out of the rubber until there is little else than water in it. When the work assumes a bright or polished appearance, wash it down as clean as possible with brush and sponge—the brush to remove all particles of pummice stone from the corners or edges of mouldings, and the sponge to absorb the water—and wipe dry with a chamois skin. Your work will then be ready for flowing.

Should you only desire to finish the wood with the flowing coat, you will, when ready, prepare it by thoroughly cleaning all floors, shelving, or anything that will catch dust or dirt, in the room, and after closing all windows, transoms and openings that would admit of a circulation of air from the outside. Then with brush and water wash the work, using great care to remove every particle of pummice stone or dust from the corners and mouldings that may not have been removed by the first washing. Wipe dry with chamois skin, as before, being careful to clean and sponge the angles of junction with work and floor, so that, in varnishing, your brush cannot possibly come in contact with any particle of dirt. When the washing is finished, sprinkle the floors, and keep them damp, to prevent dust from rising while the work is in progress.

You will then apply the best flowing varnish, made from the pure Zanzibar gum (which the writer has found to be reliable), or the best Noble's & Hoare English coach varnish, using a one inch flat fitch flowing, and a two inch brush of the same material. Commence the work as follows: First rub the
2

surface to be flowed thoroughly by drawing the palm of your
hand over it, letting the fingers clean all the small surfaces of
the angles of every particle of dust that may have settled upon
the work. Then, with your small brush, lay the varnish on
your mouldings, running entirely around the panel. When
the moulding is finished, carefully remove with a dry brush
any little saging or settling that may develop itself or accumu-
late in the corners. When you find the varnish perfectly set,
proceed in the same manner with the two inch or large brush,
to lay the varnish upon the panel until every particle of the
surface is covered. Then lay it off by carefully drawing your
nearly dry brush up and down, in order to draw out or obliter-
ate all brush marks that may be left after the first application
of varnish. Repeat this operation on each panel of the door,
until finished. In like manner, with a large No. 3-0 brush (to
be perfectly clean and free from specks), flow the low or bottom
rail of the door; then the small center rail between panels;
then the lock rail; then the center rail between two upper
panels; then the top rail; then the two side rails (bringing
them down evenly at the same time to the bottom), and your
door is finished. When you commence upon the rails, get over
them as fast as possible, to prevent your varnish from setting
at the ends of the rail joining the side, and to avoid laps of
the varnish. In flowing the side rails (and this is the reason
for doing the bottom rail first), you will work to the top, as the
work on the upper portion of the door is most seen, and
imperfections noticed, and does not show so readily at the
bottom. The writer could hardly find room on paper to state
all the different phases that occur to the workman in this one
branch of the painting business—caused by the position of the
work, the temperature of the weather, the cleanliness of the
air from minute particles, and many other things which must
be taken advantage of and be guarded against by the skill and
tact of the workman, in order to insure a perfect job of work.

The painter should at all times have with him a small cup
partly filled with varnish, and a small brush, to be used in re-
touching those parts of his work not perfectly clean, or where
he has doubts of its perfect cleanliness, such as carvings and
angles coming in contact with the floors or ceilings. He

should make it his first duty to attend to those places, so as to set or fasten particles of dirt that may not have been removed by the washings. By this precaution he will avoid soiling his brushes and prevent his varnish from becoming thick or dirty.

White walnut, oak, ash and chestnut, being of coarse, open grain, must have at least two more coats than pine or cherry. and in addition to that should have a coat of patent filling and shellac, as follows: Prime the work with a good coat of filling, and after standing a day or two to dry, give it a light coat of pure white shellac varnish. When this has become thoroughly dry, rub the surface with almost smooth sandpaper, or old pieces that have been used before. Then apply a coat of the best hard drying coach or rubbing body coach, as near full strength as you can. When this coat is thoroughly dry, again rub the surface of the varnish smooth, and repeat until you have applied at least four coats, giving as much time between each coat to dry, as the nature of your work will permit. If after applying four coats, you find that the pores or soft parts of the grain are not thoroughly filled, which will be more probable with ash, oak and chestnut (except it be veneers), sandpaper it again, and give it another coat. Rub it as before directed.

As perfect rubbing is an art only acquired by long practice and experience, I would recommend any one proposing to do a fine piece of work to first obtain the services of the best practical varnish rubber and polisher he can find, and put himself entirely under his instruction. After the work has been filled and rubbed, you should desire to polish instead of flowing the surface, give the work a flowing coat of the best piano polishing varnish, and let it dry for at least ten days. When thoroughly dry, take a cloth rubber, with pummice stone and water, and remove the top of gloss from the varnish. When perfectly smooth, again rub very carefully and thoroughly with pulverized rotten-stone and water, cleaning off and giving the final polish with the palm of the hand, which must be very soft and smooth and free from dirt or grit, as the slightest particle of either will make scratches that will ruin its appearance and necessitate the re-rubbing of the entire work.

BLACK WALNUT.

Black walnut, to give it an oil polish or French polish, as it is sometimes called, should first have a coat of patent filling well rubbed in and cleaned off. It should then have four good coats of brown shellac varnish applied at intervals of three or four days. When thoroughly dry, rub down with very fine smooth sandpaper and boiled linseed oil until you get a hard, smooth and impervious polish.

To finish without polish, first fill the grain of the wood with a coat of patent filling, and when dry, finish by rubbing oil and shellac into the wood with a cloth rubber, and adding oil and shellac until your work has a smooth, dead, solid finish, which, when well done, has a very pleasant effect in contrast with other woods that are varnished and have a high polish. It has also an advantage over the first process, as it enables the painter to finish his work at once and without delay. Both processes admit of a a great deal of practice, as the party rubbing is apt (as in the varnish) to rub through the different coats to the wood. A practical eye can at once easily detect a place that has been cut in rubbing. All other kinds of wood can be finished in oil by the same process, but light-colored woods do not look so well in oil as with the varnish finish.

VARNISHING ON PAINTED WORK.

In varnishing wood that has had paint upon it, none but the best flowing varnish should be used, and to make the work look well the painter should apply his varnish as freely as it will consistently bear, blending it out carefully and evenly. When his piece of work is finished, he should look over all the corners of mouldings and ends of panels, wiping up, with a dry brush, all runs or anything that tends to settle. When he is satisfied that the varnish has so far set as to have no further tendency to run, he will leave it to become hard and dry. Should he find in the varnish a tendency to crawl or not properly adhere to the work, as is often the case in chilly or damp weather, he will add one tablespoonful of spirits of ammonia to each pot of varnish, which will make his varnish adhere without further trouble. But he must be careful not to put too much ammonia in it, as it will make it too strong and have a tendency to mar or dampen the gloss. After the work is varnished, and has stood for three or four days, to become thoroughly dry, and you should wish it to look extra well, rub the surface of the work with haircloth until all the gloss has been removed. Then dust off well, and apply another smooth flowing coat of clean varnish. Your work will then have a polish and a durability of wear that will repay you for the trouble and cost of the extra coat. By the application of a third coat, after due time is given for the last, or second coat to dry, he will have a sufficient body of varnish to rub and polish, should he desire to go that far.

The painter will bear in mind that he can put on paint a coat every day, one over the other, until his work has received the required number of coats, and do his work no especial harm. But with varnish he will find (especially if he desire a nice job, and wishes to rub it down) that he must give it time to become perfectly dry before putting one coat upon the other; and also that he must have a sufficient number of coats (according to the nature of the wood) to enable him to do so without rubbing his work through the varnish. Pine and cherry being of a close fine grain, will look well with two coats of good extra No. 1 copal, and a last or flowing coat, while white walnut, black walnut and mahogany will require four coats and a coat of filling. Ash, oak and chestnut will require a coat of filling and four coats of hard drying or extra No. 1 copal (whichever you may choose to use), to fill them up to a sufficient surface to rub down perfectly; and frequently this is not enough to make a perfect polishing surface to work upon. In doing a nice job of this kind of work, when a polish is required, too much care cannot be taken to make it perfect.

To owners of buildings who intend using the hard-wood finish of their natural color, I would say, spare no pains in getting a first-class workman, and see that the full number of coats of the right kind of varnish is applied; also, that they are put on at the proper time and in a workmanlike manner, as it is the easiest thing in the world to entirely ruin the grain of the prettiest wood by employing inferior workmen, or by improper application.

GLAZING

Is a branch so intimately connected with the Painter's trade as to be indispensable to it. No Painter thinks of having a sign over his door without the words " Painter and Glazier," and yet not one Painter in a hundred can be called a perfect Glazier. To be a good and fast Glazier is a fine thing, and is a sure foot-hold to a steady and permanent situation, and the possessor of this accomplishment is always sure to be a favorite in the shop.

The manner of running putty on is so simple that it is unnecessary to describe the process. The Glazier must have a good, clean cut, nearly square-edged putty-knife; his putty must be well mixed, and of a consistency to be easily molded under the fingers. As practice alone will make a perfect Glazier, we leave him to graduate in that way.

CLEANING OLD VARNISH.

. No old varnish should ever be done over, or revarnished until it has been perfectly cleaned. Rub it lightly with a cloth rag and pummice stone and water, in the usual manner. Washing with soap and water will not entirely remove the smoke that always accumulates upon work that stands for any length of time in this climate. Before varnishing, the work should be well washed with a short brush and sponge, and wiped with chamois, to make it clean and free from all particles of pummice stone that may have been left on the work in cleaning. Old varnish that has been previously well done, when cleaned and varnished in this manner, has a splendid gloss, and looks a great deal better than any unrubbed work can look. The old varnish being well dried, it gives a hard, smooth foundation to finish on.

WAXING.

To wax hard woods, instead of oiling or varnishing, have the work well cleaned, using a proportion of one pound of white wax, one pound of boiled linseed oil, one pound spirits of turpentine, heated over a slow fire until reduced to a liquid state, being careful not to let it burn or become scorched. Apply with a brush or cloth, and rub well into the pores of the wood. When well filled, rub hard with corkwood until polished. Should you not succeed in perfectly filling the wood by the first application, give it a second coat, polishing off with the corkwood until the surface is smooth and hard. Should you desire to have it perfectly free from stickiness, give it a light thin coat of white shel-ac varnish, and rub smooth with haircloth until dry—always rubbing with the grain.

In waxing floors, do not use oil in the wax, but thin up entirely with spirits of turpentine, applying it as freely as possible and always while hot, as when cold it does not penetrate the wood so easily. Should too much remain upon the floor to be rubbed, remove it with a large piece of haircloth placed over a block provided with a handle. Rub until the floor is perfectly full and smooth.

To clean old floors that have been previously waxed, remove every particle of dirt by scraping with a steel scraper (such as is used by carpenters to scrape wood), and wash clean with turpentine. Rub well with the haircloth rubber, and wax as before directed.

TO PAINT BRICK WORK.

Clean it thoroughly with an old stiff broom or brush, and prime with pure yellow ochre and boiled linseed oil. When ready for the second coat, putty up all the large holes and other imperfections. If you wish to produce a light stone color, take two thirds of pure yellow ochre and one third of pure white lead, add a very little lampblack and a slight tint of Venetian red to give it a warm tint; stir well together; add, while yet thick, sufficient Japan dryer to dry it well, and mix thoroughly. Thin with raw oil to the proper thickness, and apply carefully. When ready for the third or last coat, take what you have left of the second coating, if any, and add as much lead to it as you think it will require, with yellow ochre, and a slight tint each, in very small quantities at a time, of black and Venetian red, until you have the tint desired. Apply as before instructed.

If you wish to make the cornice of a darker shade, take some of your finishing color and add red, yellow and black to it until of the required shade.

To paint a tin roof, or any metal work, I would recommend Prince's brown and pure boiled linseed oil. This being 78 per cent. pure iron and perfectly free from all acids, has more affinity for and is better adapted as a covering for all galvanized iron and tin, or other metal work, than any other pigment known. Yellow ochre and Venetian red being of pretty much the same nature, are as good, but no better; the brown having the preference on account of its fineness and great covering capacity, covering more space with the same quantity than either the red or yellow.

LEARNING THE TRADE.

To young men proposing to learn the House and Sign Painting trade, I would say, apprentice yourself to one who, from his reputation, is known to be not only a good workman, but also strictly honorable and honest in all his dealings. Go to work with the full determination of learning the business thoroughly. Do not loiter or play during working hours, though others and older persons than you do. Obey your boss to the letter; be industrious, persevering, and careful to do everything as you are instructed, and by all means endeavor to finish your entire term of apprenticeship with the man with whom you first engaged, as in this way only will you succeed in becoming perfect. When you have served your full time, work at least one year, if not two, with other good bosses, in order to become perfectly familiarized with the manner of different bosses in doing their work.

If you should desire to start the business for yourself, find a friend or acquaintance who has a house to build, make him an offer to do the painting, being sure that your offer will at least pay you reasonable days' wages. In making your estimates, be careful to ascertain what all the material and tools will cost, estimating for the very best qualities. Be particular to make a first class job of work. And by all means, whether you realize fair days' wages or not, pay every dollar of indebtedness you contract for promptly, and from the start. Show to your customers, and to those from whom your purchase stock, that you are a strictly honest and honorable man. You will find it an uphill business to push against the world, but persevere, and you will eventually succeed.

Save your earnings by investing them in a good set of tools, such as ladders, buckets, scaffold ropes, and all the different paraphernalia of a well-appointed shop. As fast as your cash accumulates beyond your wants, put it to some good and useful purpose, investing it in such material as your trade most demands. Never lose sight of the maxim upon which you base your business—to do justice to all men, no matter whether it puts money in or takes it from your purse. Should you at any time, while in business, by miscalculation or otherwise, take a job of work by which you will lose money, do not slight the work in the least on that account, but finish it just as well, and use just as good material as if it paid a profit. Show to your customer that, though you do not make anything on his work, you are not taking advantage of him. By pursuing this honest course, it will take but a few years for you to become known, and when this is accomplished, it will no longer remain an up-hill business with you. Parties will give you their work in full confidence, dealers will solicit your trade, and not only offer you credit, but will sell you their best articles at their very lowest prices.

ADULTERATIONS OF PAINTS, &c.

With many years of experience as a user and worker of paints, we have learned to think there is no white paint as durable as pure white lead combined with pure linseed oil. This is universally acknowledged as the standard of all white paints; but owing to the great competition—the result of which has been to throw upon the market vast quantities of combinations composed of different white substances, such as china, clay, whitening, zinc and sulphate of barytes—to such an extent has this system of adulteration been carried, that the question with manufacturers is not, " What can we produce as a paint that will preserve and protect from the weather?" but, " How can we produce a paint, or substitute, that will enable us to undersell our neighbor ?" The party who can produce an article the nearest resembling lead in whiteness and bulk, at the least cost of production, will, for the time, be most successful. We find it well to say here, in the language of our worthy co-worker in the paint and oil trade, Mr. BREINIG, that as the margin to the paint-grinder in the preparation of pure lead is so very small, the object is to imitate pure lead as near as possible in appearance, size of keg and working. As there is but one article that comes near to the gravity of white lead, and which is universally used for adulteration, viz : sulphate of barytes. This being a pure white, and as heavy as lead, and having no coloring power whatever, is used largely for adulterating all kinds of paint and colors. We speak conscientiously when we say we do not think one-fifth of all the lead and colors sold in the United States is perfectly free from a more or less per cent. of adulteration with this article. This article has no affinity for either lead or oil, and though you may grind it with lead and oil until it is an impalpable powder, its adhesive power will be of no more value as a covering body than so much sand, and will only act as a divider of the particles of lead and oil and make them more susceptible to the rays of the sun and the action of the weather, causing it, in a very short time, to rub off like dust. It is also perfectly useless as a preserver of the wood or other substance to which it is applied.

We would recommend those who propose painting, to at all times buy of parties in which they have perfect confidence, as there is no article of commerce so easily adulterated and so hard to detect, until practically tested, as white lead and colors. Do not buy an article represented as lead that is sold at a less rate than the regular price for the pure article. If you depart from this rule you will certainly be cheated.

GENERAL HINTS ON COMBINATION OF COLOR.

The four principal colors most used by the painters are yellow ochre, Venetian red, lampblack, and white lead, from which almost every conceivable shade of composite color can be made. All paints are mixed in exactly the same way (or at least should be);—i. e., the dryer, whether it be patent dryer or liquid, should be first perfectly mixed with the base or predominate color before it is thinned up for use, especially if the thinners used is entirely of linseed oil, as is the case for outside work. Japan mixed with color that has been first thinned to a working consistency with oil is of little use, owing to its tendency to coagulate or curdle in coming in contact with the oil, thus losing all, or nearly all, of its drying properties. It also tends to make the color look muddy, and works badly under the brush, from the large amount of gluey or curdled gum left floating on the paint from improperly mixing. Japan dryer should never be used in any delicate shade of color, nor should it be used as a dryer for white, except as a priming or first coat, owing to the darkness of its composition. The best English patent dryer is the most commonly used of any other for all white lead zinc, and for all other delicate shades of color, such as violet, ashes of roses, Paris green, pinks, &c., &c., and for the most delicate of white. In flake whites, nothing but sugar of lead should be used as a dryer; white, or zinc lead used as a base for all composite colors that partake of a gray or drab tint. To make a drab, take of white lead the fourth of the quantity you want, and after mixing in your dryer thoroughly, add yellow ochre till of a light cream color, then the slightest possible tint of Venetian red and lampblack. If not yellow enough, add yellow; if not gray enough, add a little more black; if not warm enough, add a little red; and so on until you have the shade desired. By adding either of the above colors, your tint may be made lighter or darker, and to *match any color you wish*. The same formula will answer for light, medium, or dark stone color, or for light or dark yellow drab. By letting the red and black predominate, you can produce any shade of brown color, and with pure white lead and burnt umber, you can produce the most delicate of all the drab tints.

White lead and yellow ochre will produce a very pretty shade of oak ground, and is almost entirely used for nearly all the oak graining now done.

White lead, orange chrome yellow, and a slight tint of burnt sienna, makes the most beautiful shade of color that can be produced for oak graining, and can be made lighter or darker, to suite the taste, by the addition of a proportionate quantity of chrome yellow and sienna.

The same composition, with the addition of a little English vermilion, or Venetian red, will make a very handsome shade of salmon or flesh color. White lead, with ultramarine blue, drop black, and Indian red, makes a French gray.

White lead, Indian red, with slight tint of ultramarine blue, makes violet or lavender. White lead or zinc, with carmine, makes peach blossom, and with a little cobalt blue, makes a most delicate shade of lavender. The same combination, with a little ivory black to take off the sharpness of the blue, and carmine, makes the most delicate tints of gray that can be produced. White lead, with a little lampblack, makes a lead color, and so on until, as before remarked, almost any color, or combination of colors can be produced from the proper combining of the whole with the three primary colors, red, black and yellow, or Rochelle ochre. These four ingredients, in the hands of one who is conversant with the combination and harmony of colors, is capable of producing almost as many varieties of tints as there are letters in the alphabet.

Prussian blue and chrome yellow make green; and by their proper combination, all the different shades of chrome green are made. Prussian blue, burnt umber and chrome yellow (the later to be used as the base of the color) make a very delicate shade of bronze green.

Chrome yellow and lampblack (the later added in very small quantities) will make a very pleasant shade of bronze green, and is that which is most generally used by painters in this city.

Chrome green and Venetian red in equal parts make a good groundwork for black walnut, and when stippled with umber and over-grained with Van Dyke brown in distemper, the lights wiped out with a sponge, and again over-grained with an over-grainer, make a most beautiful crotch of black walnut.

Chrome yellow and red lead makes a mahogany ground for graining, but white lead, chrome yellow and burnt sienna make the best ground for mahogany.

White lead and chrome yellow make a ground for maple or satinwood.

Venetian red and chrome yellow make a groundwork for rose-wood, though very little else than the clear Venetian red (always mixed perfectly flat, or without oil), is the article most used by painters.

Any of the above combinations will answer in distemper or water colors, in coloring walls or ceilings, and produce the same effect, with the exception that in place of white lead (which from its weight is apt to precipitate or settle), Paris white or zinc lead is used, as per formula before given.

Putty is made from pure Spanish whitening and linseed oil, kneaded like dough until hard or stiff enough for use. To make it dry quickly and hard, add a little letharge; but it is more liable to last or wear if it is set naturally or without any dryer, as it is very apt to shrink and crack off from drying too fast. All glass set in sky-lights, hot-beds, or green-houses, should be laid or bedded in putty, and well sprigged down. All superfluous putty should be cleaned out from the under side, and the space between the wood and glass on the outside neatly and smoothly pressed down to a perfect level with the glass. No putty should be used in the angles, as is commonly done, but instead, the space that is usually occupied or filled with putty, should be well traced with two good, heavy coats of white lead, yellow ochre, or red lead mixed with nothing but boiled linseed oil. The paint should be put freely in the angle of the sash-bar, or muntin (the wood portion dividing two or more lights) and glass, and should be run on to the glass as far as the putty line of the bedding shows from beneath the glass. Sash glazed in this manner, if properly painted every three or four years, will last without leaking, unless the glass is broken, for a longer time than by the old process.

Spanish whiting, red lead, and litharge, combined in equal parts, makes a putty that will dry and harden under water, and is used for glazing aquariums and all other vessels used to hold water.

BRUSHES.

The brushes mostly in use by the practical painter are of the round kinds—the 5-0, 6-0, 7-0. A few of them who like a very large brush, use the 8-0 paint brush.

The sash-tool most used are the French sash, and of the Nos. 5, 6, 7 and 8; the latter being the largest size generally used. The flat or paste brushes most used are the three and a half inch, mostly used by grainers for rubbing in their color, and the four and five inch by the painter, for brick work, and for all large surfaces. These brushes are all made of three qualities (except sash-tools and varnish-tools, which are made wholly from white bristles). The qualities of bristles are as follows: The best or Okatka (the name is derived from the place of production) ; the bristles are all white, and are long, stiff, but very flexible. These are put into the most expensive brushes. The second quality is composed of an outer coating of say one third all white bristles, and the inner two-thirds of all gray bristles. The third, or common quality, is composed of a very small outer coating of white bristles of any kind, so they are long enough, and the balance of the space filled with Tampico hemp—a very long, stiff, white grass largely imported from Mexico and the West India Islands. This latter brush is made only for the country trade, and cannot be sold to any one who has had experience in the handling of a paint brush. As all painters, or those who have had any experience, know their uses, as also their difference in quality, we will pass them by, and again refer to varnishes.

VARNISHES RESUMED.

There are eight kinds of varnish used in house-painting, as follows: Asphaltum or black varnish, used for backing grate fronts, and all kinds of iron work. It is sometimes used, when diluted with spirits of turpentine, as a stain to imitate black walnut. No. 1 copal, or cheap furniture varnish, composed of gum, resin, linseed oil, spirits of turpentine, is of very little use, except as a cheap article with which to demoralize the market and spoil good wood-work. Extra No. 1 copal or furniture, made of the pure gum copal (entirely a foreign product, none of it ever having been found in this country), pure linseed oil and spirits of turpentine boiled to a very high degree of heat. This is the only varnish used by furniture makers who have any pretensions to the turning out of a good and well-finished article. The next of the class is the hard-drying or rubbing body coach varnish, made from the same but more carefully selected gum. Linseed oil and turpentine are used as the foundation coats of all coach bodies, and for all finest class house work finished with the natural wood, and is made for the express purpose from which it derives its name, to be rubbed down to a polishing surface. It is not good as a finishing or last coating varnish, as it is a very hard dryer, which has a tendency to deaden its gloss.

Flowing varnish is the next best quality, and is made of the very best quality of Zanzibar, with the proportions of oil and turpentine so nicely blended as to make it set or dry in just the time necessary to render it a perfect piece of work. It is the varnish with which all nice furniture is finished, and derives its name from its use, as it is always put on or flowed as freely as it can possibly be done without running or sagging.

Finishing coach body is the next best class of varnish, and, like the flowing, is made of the very best material, the one exception being that the oil is more perfectly boiled and clarified, and there is less turpentine in it than any other varnish, which makes it dry much slower. This varnish is used as the last or finishing coat for all coach bodies, and for all other wood or iron work upon which varnish is put as a preservative and beautifier.

The English coach has, so far, from the same cause, borne the best reputation as a wearing and durable varnish, and is largely sold and used in this country by all who desire to produce good work.

The next varnish used by the house-painter is Damar varnish, and is composed of gum Damar and spirits of turpentine, and can be made either cold or hot, though the heating of the turpentine to about 175 to 190 degs. (not higher, as the gas arising from turpentine at a much higher degree is apt to ignite), makes a much quicker and better mixed varnish, and is composed of about four pounds of gum to the gallon of turpentine. This varnish is principally used to varnish all light-colored papers and delicate wall tints, and is the varnish from which, with the addition of French zinc, the porcelain or enamel white is made. When well and properly made, it produces the prettiest white finish ever used in house painting.

Our next, and very useful varnish, is made from gum lac or shellac, as it is commonly called. This is made from alcohol spirits of 96 per cent. proof, as no less will perfectly dissolve it, and is made by adding three to four pounds of shellac to the gallon, and agitating it until entirely dissolved or taken up by the spirits. This varnish is what our oiled furniture or French polishers finish with (as before described), and is capable of being finished very beautifully. It is also called knotting varnish, being used as a substitute to kill knots. Pine wood that is to be finished a gloss white or porcelain finish, should always have a coat of shellac varnish before a particle of paint is put on it.

Lastly, comes the most useful of all—the Japan varnish or dryer. This varnish or dryer enters into the every day consumption of the painter to such an extent, and is so universally known, that we will pass it by, with our compliments for its usefulness.

CONCLUDING REMARKS.

We did think we would say something in this little treatise on the plain facts about painting, but we have now extended our little book much further, and said a great deal more than we intended. We should like to have said something about the application of paints to prevent cracking or blistering. As also something in regard to the combination and harmony of tints of color in the decorating of walls and ceilings. We cannot, however, close without saying a word or two about the varnishing of paper, which has lately become so prevalent.

VARNISHING PAPER.

To varnish a delicate tinted paper, and preserve its normal color, great care must be taken in preparing and applying the size. Take of the best A extra white glue, as much as you think you will require to give your work two good coats of size. Let it soak for an hour, or over night, in cold water. Then set your pail of soaked glue into a kettle of boiling water, first pouring off the cold water remaining unabsorbed by the glue, and replacing it with boiling water. Stir until entirely dissolved; then dilute with cold water until of proper consistency, apply carefully with a very soft six or eight-inch coloring brush, touching the paper as lightly as possible, and at the same time spreading the size as evenly as you can, until you have given the entire surface of the paper one coat. Let this coat get well dried, and, after thickening your size, go over the paper again, giving it a thorough coat, spreading the color right and left, and laying it off up and down. When dry, give it a good coat of pure white Damar varnish, being careful to have it thinned to its proper consistency. Before you finish each stretch or panel of the work, if the tint will stand the test, and not change its color, you will improve your varnish by adding about a pint to the gallon of the best pale finishing coach varnish, as Damar varnish alone is not a very durable or wearing varnish, and is easily rubbed off. For all dark papers, like oak or walnut, any varnish that you would use on grained work will do. and in fact is better for the work than any other.

ITEMS OF INTEREST TO THE PAINTER.

Vermilion is a French word which signifies *worm-dye*, and was originally so called from the fact that the color was first produced from the dried bodies of a species of small insects, called kermes, who feed upon the oaks in the vicinity of the Mediterranean Sea. Hence, *vermilion* has come to be the name of all red colors of its class, even those which are produced from minerals.

The vermilion of antimony was invented in 1833 by Lampodias, and consists of a red sulphuret of antimony, in the form of a very fine, inodorous and insipid powder, insoluble in water, alcohol and spirits, and subject to but little change by contact with the weak acids, or by the strong mineral acids. It is, moreover, but little affected by ammonia and alkaline carbonates; but the strong alkalies, potash and caustic soda, affect it more or less, by combining. The vermilion of antimony cannot, therefore, be mixed with colors which have an alkaline reaction, nor will it withstand a high degree of heat, but will blacken under such influence.

Vermilion is an opaque color. When moistened with water, or mixed with gum or gelatine, it has no lustre, but when combined with oil or varnish it becomes exceedingly brilliant and intense in color. It covers well and surpasses in this respect all mineral colors. It presents, perhaps, *the very purest hue of red*, a hue which never turns orange or crimson, though it generally retains a slight tint of brown. Vermilion is not favorable to the drying of oil, although it does not retard its drying to any great degree.—*Coach Maker's Magazine.*

INJURIOUS EFFECTS OF TURPENTINE.

Experience has taught that the so-called lead paralysis, common among painters, in the form of a loss of motion of the wrist joints, is chiefly produced by the habit of washing the hands in turpentine. It is probable that it is not the turpentine alone which produces this fatal result, but chiefly the particles of lead or zinc paint on the hands which, by the turpentine, are brought in a condition to penetrate the skin more readily and to be absorbed; therefore, painters should avoid, as much as possible, the use of turpentine for washing the hands.

WHITE LEAD.

The *Scientific American* recommends the following as the best means of testing the purity of white lead ground in oil : Take a small portion and wash it with spirits of turpentine, to remove the oil, and rinse thoroughly with alcohol. Pour on the sample thus prepared dilute nitric acid. If a residue remains, it is sufficient indication of sulphate of baryta. The weight of this substance when separated from the solution by filtering and drying. will, when compared with the weight of the sample, give the proportion of this very common adulteration, provided sulphate of lead be not present. The clear solution which has been filtered

3

off, may next be tested for carbonate of lime (chalk or whiting), by evaporating to dryness and treating with alcohol. This will dissolve the nitrate of lime into which the carbonate of lime has been changed by the first treatment with nitric acid. The loss of weight in the residue after treatment with the alcohol, filtering, and drying, will indicate the proportion of carbonate of lime present in lead, provided there is no oxide of zinc present; and the amount of carbonate of lime may be determined by multiplying this loss by 56 and dividing the product by 82; the quotient will be the weight of carbonate of lime present in the sample before treatment.

A mixture of lead, carbonate and oxide of zinc, prepared cheaply from an ore found in North Carolina, has been latterly used to adulterate white lead; therefore, oxide of zinc may be present. To test for this salt, add to the alcoholic solution obtained in the first washing, sulphide of ammonium, which will throw down all the zinc as a sulphide, five-sixths of which will be the amount of oxide of zinc present in the sample, which must be deducted in estimating the carbonate of lime. Sulphate of lead may be present; if so, it will remain undisturbed with the sulphate of baryta, upon the first treatment with nitric acid. It may be washed entirely out of the sulphate of baryta with pure water; the loss in weight ascertained after drying the sulphate of baryta, will then indicate the quantity of sulphate of lead present. In this case the whole of the residue at first left when the nitric acid is added is not the sulphate of baryta, and the latter must be weighed after washing out the lead salt.

TO BLEACH SHELLAC.

Dissolve in an iron kettle one part of pearlash in eight parts of water; add one part of pulverized shellac or seed lac, and heat the whole to ebullition. When the lac is dissolved, cool the solution and impregnate it with "chlorine" till the lac is precipitated This precipitate is white, but its color is deepened by washing and consolidation. Dissolve in alcohol. Lac bleached by this process yields a varnish as clear as opal.

HOW COMMON WINDOW GLASS IS MADE.

If ever you visit Pittsburg, in Pennsylvania, you must go into the window glass factories there; you will find them very curious.

Their furnace, in the first place, is built in the ancient style; it has no chimney, and the smoke from the bituminous coal they burn, pours out in a cloud into the room. There are openings in the roof for it to escape through, and a continual draught of air from the doors carries it upward, so that it is not so bad for the workmen as one would think. Besides, they do not begin to blow off until the smoke is all burnt off.

There are five pots on each side of the furnace; and you will see five men in a row, blowing all at once, with the regularity of a file of soldiers exercising. Each gathers 30 or 40 pounds of metal on his pipe, which is very long and strong. They stand on platforms, to get room to swing the glass, as they blow it. The five men begin to blow and swing all together. Each blows a great globe of glass, which is stretched out gradually by the swinging motion into a cylinder or roller, as it is called, five feet long. Then the five rollers are swung up toward the furnace holes, and five other soldiers spring forward with their guns, —which in this case are iron bars—that they set upright under the five blowing pipes to support them while the rollers are being reheated in the necks of the pots. The blowers blow in the necks of the pipes with all their might, then clap their thumbs over the holes to prevent the air from rushing out again; in the meanwhile the end of the roller is softened, so that at last the air, forced in and expanded by the heat, bursts it outward. The glass is then a cylinder, open at one end. It is whirled in the heat until the edges become true, then brought away—the five iron supports dropping to the ground with a simultaneous clang. The cylinders are laid on tables, where the imperfect spherical end about the blowing pipe is cracked off from the rest by a strip of melted glass drawn around it. The cylinder is then cracked from end to end on one side by means of a red hot iron passed through it.

In the adjoining building is what is called the flattening oven. The cylinders brought there are lifted on the end of a lever, passed in through a circular opening just large enough to admit them, and laid on flattening stones on the oven bottom, with the crack uppermost. The oven bottom is circular, and it revolves horizontally. As the glass softens, it separates at the crack, and lays itself down gently and gradually on the stone.

The long cylinder is then a flat sheet, three feet wide and nearly five feet in length. There are four openings around the sides of the oven; at one the glass is put in, through another a workman sweeps the stone for it, a third workman smooths it down with a block as it comes round to him, and a fourth, at the last opening, which is close to the one at which it was put in, lifts the sheet—partly cooled by this time—upon a carriage in the oven. This he does by means of a lever furnished with sharp, broad blades at the end, which he works in under the glass. When the carriage is full, it is run through an annealing oven beyond,

The opposite end of the annealing oven opens into the cutting room. There the carriages are pushed along a central track. and unloaded at the stalls of the cutters. The cutter has a table before him, with measure marks on its edges. He lifts one of the sheets, lays it on a table, and commences ruling it faster than a school boy rules his slate. His ruler is a wooden rod, five feet long, and his pencil point is a diamond. Every stroke is a cut. Not that he cuts the glass quite apart; indeed he seems only to make a scratch. Yet that scratch has the effect of cracking the glass quite through, so that it breaks clean off at the slightest pressure. In this way the sheets are cut up into panes of the required size.

I remember, one workman told me that a single diamond would last him two or three years. It has fifteen or sixteen different edges, and when one edge is worn out he uses another. South American diamonds, such as he uses, cost, he told me, from six to thirty dollars each; and when they are worn out for his purpose, he sells them for jewels to be put into watches.—[*J. T. Trowbridge.*

CAUSES OF PAINT CRACKING AND FLAKING.

The cracking and flaking of paint has always been a source of trouble to the carriage manufacturer. As a rule, the painter or the varnishmaker have had to bear all the blame; there is no doubt but they, in too many instances, are responsible, but it is not right that they should be made the scapegoats for the faults of others, or for causes beyond their control. There are a great many theories concerning the cracking and falling off of paint, but as a rule, these theories are false to a greater or less extent. To no one cause can this trouble be rightfully charged, but with this, as with everything else, there is a leading cause that over-shadows all others, and which will produce the result, even if every other cause were removed, although possibly not to the same extent, and a few words in relation to this greatest and most destructive cause will not be out of place.

All paint that is to be put upon bare wood is, or should be, mixed with vegetable oil; this oil is the life of the paint which it mixes, and when this is absorbed in any manner from the paint it loses all life and becomes worthless. All kinds of wood will expand and contract when exposed to the atmosphere, according as the moisture is dryer than the wood; while the paint retains the oil this expansion or contraction does it no injury, but when the wood has absorbed the oil, which it will do in time, the paint loses its elasticity and becomes a thin, hard shell, and can no longer accommodate itself to the action of the wood; the expansion of the wood, therefore, causes it to crack, and as the wood contracts it is again forced together, until, by continual action of this kind, it becomes loosened from the wood and flakes off. Take, for instance, a carriage wheel after the wood has absorbed the oil from the lead and the paint has cracked, and strike a quick blow upon a spoke, and see how quick the paint will flake off. A few experiments of this kind will convince any one that the lead or pigments forming the paint have no vitality after the oil has been absorbed from them. We presume that there are very few persons who will dispute the fact that wood will absorb the oil; if there are such let them experiment a little and they will soon become convinced of their error. They would find their experience the same as that of a painter who had spent many years in the shop and carefully studied causes and effects. He said: "I primed a set of wheels with oil, and when sufficiently dry, sandpapered them and gave them a coat of the best B. B. English lead, mixed with a large proportion of oil; when dry 1 puttied them up and sandpapered them, and gave them another coat of lead, then finished them in the usual manner. I saw the carriage some time after, and some portions of the paint had flaked off, and in those places the wood had so completely absorbed the oil that, had I not known that oil priming had been used, and that there was a large portion of oil in the lead, I should not have had an idea that oil had been used."

The best and purest lead will retain the oil the longest, hence it will resist the action of the wood in absorbing it for the greatest length of time, and in proportion to its adulteration it loses its power and tenacity to retain the oil and resist its absorption by the wood. Remember this, you who buy pure lead because it is cheap, and do not blame the unfortunate painter who is compelled to use it.—*Harness and Carriage Journal.*

BRUSH MAKING.

There is almost no end to the variety of brushes used in the present age; but all the various styles perform some important office in the economy of civilized life. Brushes are made of a good many kinds of materials; but bristles are the chief reliance of the brush maker in their manufacture. The principal source of supply of bristles is Russia, from whence vast quantities are exported to various countries. England, it is said, alone consumes annually over two million pounds of bristles, obtained from Russia, in addition to vast supplies of her own, and considerable quantities grown elsewhere.

Bristles, as they come off the hog's back, are covered with dirt and a sort of gummy substance, that make them very unpleasant to handle. To rid them of these, and also of offensive odors, they are first thoroughly washed, and after becoming dry are sorted. Each color is placed by itself, and these grades are known to the operative as black, grey, white, and lilies; the latter are a kind almost transparently white, and of exceedingly fine texture. The sorting process also consists of distributing the bristles in such a way that the collection shall be of equal length. Besides, the root ends of the bristles must be kept together. The next process is to comb them. By this means they are rendered elastic, and receive a beautiful polish. After being again washed, they are ready for the use of the brush maker.

Brushes are divided into two general classes, known as single brushes and compound brushes. The former are distinguished by one tuft, or bundle of bristles. But a hair brush belongs to the second order, because of its collection of bristle bundles.

Brushes are also made of the soft hair of animals, such as the sable, badger, and squirrel. Of such are the small paint brushes used for water colors. Other kinds of brushes are made of roots and fibers of certain tropical plants, of horse and goat hair, old rope, cocoanut fiber, broom corn, the fiber of whalebone, and even spun glass.

Small paint brushes are manufactured as follows: The hairs are first cleaned in alum water, and subsequently soaked in warm water, dried, combed, and assorted. The brush maker takes sufficient of the prepared hair to fill a small groove which holds them tight; while thus placed, the root ends are wound tightly with thread. The soft hairs are then arranged so as to form a point, without leaving a blunt or scraggy end when the brush is wet. This part of the business is generally performed by women or boys, as it requires a very delicate touch to arrange them properly. The handles are made from quills, which are soaked in hot water to swell them sufficiently. When the brush is ready, the hairs are inserted point first, in the large end of the quill. Then, by a contrivance peculiar to the trade, the brush is drawn through until the tied part is brought down to the small end of the quill. This completes the process, and when the quill gets cold it contracts to its original dimensions, and thus secures the brush part very tightly. The quills used for handles are of various sizes, and are obtained from geese, turkeys, ducks, and even smaller birds, such as quails, larks, &c. The size of the handle is always proportioned to the size of the brush, and the purposes for which it is made. When the quantity of hair or bristles is larger than can be used to advantage with quills, the bunch of material is put in the tube with wooden handles. Even these, when too large, are placed in handles made of wood, with perated holes. Bundles of bristles designed for this purpose are secured with strong cord, which has been dipped in glue.

Hair brushes are of the most complicated manufacture. Holes large enough to admit the bunches of bristles are bored all over the back of the brush part way through; while much smaller holes are bored clear through. A tuft of bristles is doubled over a piece of fine wire. After being thus properly secured, the workmen put the wire in the small hole, and draw the bristles up as far as possible in the big hole. The wire is then carried on to the next hole, until the whole surface is covered over with connecting lines of wire and tufts of bristles. When thus far completed, the bristles are cut off evenly, and a fancy back is glued on to hide the wire, and give the brush a more finished appearance. Tooth and nail brushes are made in a similar way, but the holes where the wire is secured are made on the side, and corked up with small plugs of ivory or bone. Some brushes have handles of perfumed wood, and are ornamented considerably, at heavy expense. Brushes made of spun glass are used in acids, which will destroy ordinary brushes.—[*New York Mercantile Journal.*

GUM-COPAL AND COPAL VARNISH.

The copal Zanzibar is the only article convertible into the fine varnishes now so extensively used throughout the civilized world. It is the product of a tree which still grows there, and the gum is found in two conditions—in a soft state, attached to the tree; and buried in the soil, where it has become hard as it is commonly seen in trade.

The tree is found on the island and mainland of Zanzibar. It is by no means as some have supposed, a shrubby thorn, its towering bole has formed canoes sixty feet long, and a single tree has sufficed for the kelson of a bridge. The average size, however, is about half that height, with from three to six feet girth near the ground. The bark is smooth; the lower branches are within reach of a man's head. The trunk is of a yellow whitish tinge, rendering it conspicuous among the dark African jungle growths; it is dotted with exudations of raw gum, which is also found scattered in bits around the base; and is infested by ants, especially by a long ginger colored and semi-transparent variety, called by the people "boiling water," from its fiery bite. The copal wood is yellow tinted, and the saw collects from it large flakes; when dried and polished, it darkens to a honeyed brown, and being well veined, it is used for the panels of doors. The modern *habitat* of the tree is the alluvial sea plain, and the anciently raised beach; though extending over the crest of the latter formation, it ceases to be found at any distance beyond the land water counter slope, and it is unknown in the interior.

The raw copal is either picked from the tree, or is found shallowly imbedded in the loose soil. To the eye, it is smoky or clouded inside; it feels soft; it becomes like putty when exposed to the action of alcohol, and it viscidizes in the solution used for washing the true copal. Little valued in European technology, it is exported to Bombay, where it is converted into an inferior varnish for carriages and palanquins, and to China, where the people have discovered, it is said, for utilizing it, a process which, like the manufacture of rice paper and Indian ink, they keep secret. Its juice varies from 12 to 27 cents a pound.

The true or ripe copal is the product of *vast extinct forests, overthrown in former ages;* and the gum has been set free by some violent action of the elements; or, it had exuded from the roots of the trees by an abnormal action which exhausted and destroyed them. The gum, buried at depths beyond atmospheric influence, has, like amber and similar gum resins, been bituminized in all its purity, the volatile principles being fixed by moisture and by the exclusion of external air. That it is the produce of a tree is proved by the discovery of pieces of gum imbedded in a touchwood which crumbles under the fingers; the "goose skin," which is the impress of sand or gravel, shows that it was buried in a soft state, and the bees, flies, gnats, and other insects which are sometimes found in it, delicately preserved, seem to disprove a remote geologic antiquity. At the end of the rains, it is usually carried ungarbled (unassorted and uncleaned) to Zanzibar. At Zanzibar, after being sifted and freed from heterogenous matter, it is sent to the Indian market or sold to the foreign merchant. It is then washed several times in soda ley. The Americans export the gum uncleaned, because the operation is better performed at Salem. Of late years they have begun to prepare it at Zanzibar, like the Hamburg traders. When taken from the ley, in which from 20 to 37 per ct. is lost, the gum is washed, sun-dried for some hours, and cleaned with a hard brush, which must not, however, injure the goose skin; the dark "eyes" where the dirt has sunk deep, are also picked out with an iron tool. It is then carefully sorted, with due regard to color and size. There are many tints and peculiarities, known only to those whose interest compel them to study and observe copal, which like cotton and Cashmere shawls, requires years of experience. The sizes are fine, medium and large, with many subdivisions; the pieces vary from the dimensions of small pebbles to two or three ounces; they have been known to weigh five pounds, and it is said at Salem a piece of thirty-five pounds is shown.

Copal is preferred to other gum resins for making varnish, on account of its hardness. It does not dissolve in water or common alcohol, even when boiling hot; and oil of turpentine dissolves only one or two per cent. of it. When heated over a quick fire, it melts into a thin fluid, and in this state it can be mixed intimately with linseed oil and spirits of turpentine. Such a mixture, with the addition of a little litharge or dried sugar of lead, constitutes copal varnish. Great care and skill are required in manufacture, to avoid accidents from fire, and to produce varnish of a good quality.

A NEW ZINC PAINT.

According to the *Comtes Rendus*, M. Artus, of the Vieille Montagne Company, France, has introduced a valuable white zinc paint, using silicate of potash instead of oil as a vehicle. It is said to be very durable, and to keep zinc metal roofing very cool; thus furnishing a paint for zinc surfaces, the want of which has been long felt. The details of the preparation are not given, but if the paint prove as valuable as seems to be anticipated, it will doubtless be introduced ere long into this country.

The Titusville *Herald* mentions the following concerning a patent process recently exhibited in Titusville by Mr. B. O'Brien, of Lockport, N. Y., for manufacturing a paint oil from petroleum, which was claimed to fully equal the linseed oil for mixing paints. Mr. O'Brien demonstrated the process to a number of refiners in Titusville, but his negotiations for the sale of the patent here was suspended by a call to New York, and a sale was effected to parties in that city. The purchasers pay $75,000 for three fourths of the patent, and furnish the requisite capital to manufacture at least one hundred barrels of the oil per day. Mr. O'Brien receives $25,000 cash in hand, and $2 per barrel on all oil sold until the balance, $50,000, is paid. He also retains a one fourth interest in the business, receiving one fourth of the net profits.

Mr. James B. Pollock, of Port Richmond, N. Y., has invented and patented an apparatus for feeding white lead, etc., from the mixing tub to the millstones. This invention consists of a feeder or conveyor for oily and pasty substances, of which the essential features are a longitudinally grooved cylinder, inclosed in a cylindrical case, and a scraper, arranged in such manner that the paste is forced from the mixer or a hopper into the groove of the cylinder at one side of the case, and carried thereby to the other side, where it is taken out by the scraper, which is caused to drop into the groove, and discharged upon any receiver, preferably a revolving disk, from which it may be discharged by a fixed scraper to any other receiver or conveyor. The case serves as a cut off to remove any excess of the paste, and cause the feed to be regular and even, being the exact quantity the grooves are capable of taking; but the quantity discharged may be varied by varying the speed of the cylinder, or by limiting the discharging scraper into the grooves, so that it will not take out the whole quantity contained in them.

PAINT AS A PROTECTOR.

Paint, in the view of utility, is employed as a protective covering to a body, against the injurious influences of the air, water, and other destructive agencies. Wood and the common metals are especially attacked by oxygen contained in our atmosphere, of which it constitutes about 21 per cent., being the 21-100 part of the whole atmosphere. It is also a component part of water, forming nearly 88-100 of its whole weight. Although its presence is absolutely necessary to the continuance of animal life, yet metals exposed to the air are consumed by the oxygen as in a fire. The utility, therefore, of paint as a protector is so apparent that any study of its composition and properties, which will tend to improve it in any degree, is of great importance.

Paint is understood to be a mixture of a liquid and a solid, in powder. The desirable physical conditions of these are, that the liquid should have a certain amount of viscidity, in order to maintain the powder in suspension, and that the powder should be as fine as possible, and nearly of the same specific gravity of the liquid. Linseed oil is undoubtedly the best mixture for paints that are to be exposed to the weather. It absorbs oxygen, and becomes solid and water-proof, and yet it always possesses some elasticity which prevents it from cracking. Theory and the almost united voice of practical painters, after centuries of experience, have decided that, in view of its inherent properties and its cost, nothing at present known can take its place. There may be special uses of paint, where some other article may be substituted with advantage, yet we cannot reasonably look beyond the class of substances known as drying oils, for a substitute. Volatile oils, and such as resin oils, which oxydize into brittle resins, are altogether out of the question. Nor will any solution or mixture of India-rubber or gutta percha take the place of linseed oil, by reason of expense as well as their inferior properties. Linseed oil, therefore, is the very best liquid for paint. Of the solids used for paint, we may mention lampblack, white lead, red lead, ver-milion, verdigris, ochres, &c., a certain combination of the dif-ferent substances in proper proportions give the various colors of brown, purple, chocolate, &c. Now the chemical properties of ingredients used in paint are of great importance. The liquid and solid must be such as will not injuriously react on each other, and such as are not destroyed by contact with air and water. The main virtue of paint resides in the liquid; the solid serves unfavorably to dilute that virtue, and favorably by secur-ing that kind of consistency which permits easy manipulation with the brush, and favorably, also, by preventing the absorption of the liquid when the paint is spread on porous surfaces.

As a theoretical question, the choice of the solid body in paint is a difficult one; it involves some of the nicest refinements of chemistry; but as a practical question, the inherent differences of the multitude of admissible substances are slight enough to bring it to the narrow consideration of cost. That substance which is permanent under ordinary influences, and which can be pow-dered and ground with oil, at the lowest cost, will be preferred. Do not the *ochres* answer to this condition? We suggest here, that metallic oxydes and carbonates generally have a certain affinity for oil, which renders the mixture more easy and inti-mate, so that the resulting dried paint is more compact and less disturbed by friction. The peculiar property of white lead, in mixing with oil, and such paint drying up to become a remarka-bly hard and tough body, is well understood, and indicates it— notwithstanding its greater cost over ochres and other cheap substances—as the best material for inside work which is to be exposed to much friction. Lead paint, however, is not suitable for surfaces much exposed to the weather. The ochres are re-commended for outside work.

PRUSSIAN BLUE.

The substance which generally affords the blue color, affords a great variety of shades. In regard to durability, the blues possess one marked characteristic, namely: those which are the purest and most brilliant are the most durable. The blue colors which are used most extensively in painting, are ultramarine, cobalt, Prussian blue, indigo, the different species of azure, etc. In the present article, we shall speak only of the third in this class.

Prussian blue was discovered in 1720, by Diesbach, in Berlin, and since that time it has been carefully studied by many chemists and manufacturers, so that its composition and preparation are well understood. It is the chemical combination of the gaseous substance known as cyanogen, with iron under two different kinds of oxidation, that is to say, protocyanide and sesquicyanide of iron and a little water. The proportions are variable, and from this cause the color varies, and colors of very different degrees of intensity are found in commerce.

In the ordinary variety, 3 parts of protocyanide and 2 parts of sesquicyanide of iron are combined with 9 parts of water.

Moreover, the method of making, the quality of the materials employed, and the care used, all exert an important influence on the color. When pure and newly precipitated, its color is so deep as to appear black, and later it looks black-blue with a slight reddish tint.

In order to obtain it pure, a preparation consisting of carbonate of potash, calcined with animal matter (usually blood), is added to the blue during the manufacture. We give a brief description of the process of making Prussian blue, as denoted by Borct. The blood is first prepared by heating in a basin and evaporating until it becomes viscid, when it is spread upon tables and exposed to the sun until dry, and it is then pulverized. Ten parts of this are taken, and a solution composed of 1 part of carbonate of potash, 1-100 part of iron filings and a little water. These ingredients are inclosed in a melting-pot which is kept at a red heat for seven or eight hours. During the first part of this process, a large quantity of offensive steam separates, which is succeeded by a light red flame. The matter is then stirred, and when it has reached a state of tranquil fusion and emits no more gases, the pot is again covered and heated for another hour. The product obtained is in the form of a cake, which is next washed with hot water until all the soluble portion has been absorbed.

This liquid, which is bright yellow and smells very strongly of prussic acid, is not pure cyanuret of potassium, but must be filtered and concentrated. After this is done, it is poured, little by little, into a warm solution of one part of alum and seven or eight parts of sulphate of iron, and it gives the color which is known as Prussian blue. When pure it is sometimes known as China or Chinese blue.

According to the authority of Mr. Burgeois, who was superintendent of a great color factory in France, Prussian blue, next to ultra-marine coblat, affords the purest shade of blue, and though inferior in this respect to these two colors, it surpasses both of them in its wonderful coloring power. Unfortunately, it cannot withstand the action of alkalies, and when combined with a color which contains an alkali, it is liable to change in a very short time, or even to lose its color entirely. It is deep-toned, brilliant, and transparent, possessing the greatest intensity of any of the blues, and in composition it gives the greatest variety of shades. When mixed with white lead, Prussian blue acquires a somewhat greenish shade. Very beautiful colors may be produced by mixing it with 15 or 20 parts (in weight) of chronium yellow, but greens so made are not durable. To obtain a sky-blue, add 1 part of Prussian blue to 20 parts of white, and for a light azure, add 1 part of same to 200 parts of white. When mixed with oil, Prussian blue should be used soon, else it will become greasy and difficult to work. The cheaper kinds are sometimes adulterated with chalk, china, clay, or starch. When mixed with chalk or other carbonates of lime, their presence may be easily tested by treating the color with an acid, which will cause the adulteration to effervesce. If starch is added, it will become pasty when mixed with boiling water.

www.ingramcontent.com/pod-product-compliance
Lightning Source LLC
Chambersburg PA
CBHW032116080426
42733CB00008B/961